TICKET ◆ TO THE ◆ TWENTIES

A Time Traveler's Guide

by

MARY BLOCKSMA

Illustrated by

SUSAN DENNEN

Little, Brown and Company
Boston New York London Toronto

To all twenties children,
especially those
who shared their childhoods with me
for this book:

Ralph and Ruth Blocksma
Bonnie Bovard
Jean and Will Clelland
Barbara and William Dunnington
Frieda Enss
Jacob Eppinga
Harold Hartger
Charles Northup
Hilda Schadel
Mary Lee Taliaferro
J. Benjamin Verhoek

First Edition

Library of Congress Cataloging-in-Publication Data
Blocksma, Mary.
        Ticket to the twenties : a time traveler's guide / Mary Blocksma :
    illustrated by Susan Dennen. —1st ed.
        p.   cm.
    Includes bibliographical references and index.
    Summary: Allows the reader to "travel" back to the 1920s, experience life as a typical young person of that time and witness some of that decade's important events.
        ISBN 0-316-09974-0
        1. United States —Social life and customs— 1918–1945—Juvenile literature.
    2. History, Modern—20th century—Juvenile literature.
    [1. United States—Social life and customs— 1918–1945. 2. United States—History— 1919–1933.] I. Dennen, Susan, ill. II. Title.
    E 169.B638   1993
    973.91 —dc20   92-24303

10 9 8 7 6 5 4 3 2 1

KP

Published simultaneously in Canada by Little, Brown & Company (Canada) Limited

Printed in the United States of America

CONTENTS

4

YOUR TICKET

Get your ticket while it's hot! Take Time Line's good-time tour of the twenties and discover a great vacation hideaway in the early twentieth century.

World War I is over, and everybody's celebrating! Enjoy our complimentary trunkful of getups; pocket a generous travel allowance; learn some new "lip." Zip back seventy years or so (return fare guaranteed) on our amazing Time Liner.

Receive a "darb" new hairstyle, stay with a twenties family, play twenties games, ride streetcars, see movies for a dime, go on shopping sprees, enjoy fun fads and thrilling inventions, and help celebrate some stunning twenties heroes, including the first man to fly solo across the Atlantic, the first woman to swim the English Channel, and one of the most incredible baseball players ever!

WHAT'S THE CATCH? To enjoy this Twenties Tour Package, you will need to learn some twenties smarts, for if your true identity is discovered, you will have to return to the present immediately. We've provided you with plenty of twenties disguises, however, and lots of advice to help you stay undetected. As long as you do, you're likely to make it all the way to the end of the decade!

DON'T KNOW WHAT A WORD MEANS?
Look it up in your special Jive Talk Twenties Dictionary on pages 18 and 19.

YOUR TRUNK

Before you leave, choose a twenties disguise from your trunk:

Dr. Dentons or nightgown

hat

school frock

party frock

corduroy knicker suit

jacket

cardigan sweater

Jive Dictionary

bloomers

knee socks

hair ribbon

travel allowance

good coat and muff

high-top shoes

patent leather shoes

handkerchiefs

golf cap

Sunday knicker suit

corduroy knicker suit

Dr. Dentons or nightshirt

good coat

detachable collar and cuffs

white shirt

Jive Dictionary

sweater

suspenders

knee socks

2 ties

jackknife

oxford shoes

travel allowance

high-top shoes

handkerchiefs

Dare to be a tourist!

It's worth toting this rather hefty Kewpie Kamera, even if it does weigh almost two pounds and uses only black-and-white film. Small, light cameras are still mostly unknown.

SNEAK IN SOME MODERN CONVENIENCES!

You might want to slip in a few things that are hard to find in the twenties — just be sure no one spots them!

soft toilet paper

sneakers

deodorant

ballpoint pen

Walkman and tapes

Band-Aids

jeans

CLOTHES

The best time to travel the twenties is spring or summer, when twenties fashions are truly "the berries" — some of the smartest in this century. Cold weather clothing, on the other hand, itches and looks lumpy, mostly because twenties mothers insist that both girls and boys wear long woolen underwear and black stockings. We provide both to all winter travelers, with apologies for any discomfort and some advice for getting them on:

HOW TO GET STOCKINGS OVER LONG UNDERWEAR. Put on a full suit of "longies" (also called a union suit), and button up the flap in the back. To get a thin black stocking over the thick white longie leg, fold a longie leg tightly behind your ankle with one hand while you pull the stocking over it with the other. This usually takes several tries!

USE YOUR HIGH-TOPS TO ANCHOR YOUR UNDERWEAR. Everyday shoes, which are the same for boys and girls, are brown leather, hard-soled, and high-topped. They're good for just one thing: If you tie them tightly around the ankle fold, they'll keep your long underwear from riding up under your socks.

CHOOSE ELASTIC BANDS TO HOLD UP YOUR STOCKINGS. The only other option is an ugly suspenderlike hose harness!

First zipper

A TWENTIES FIRST

1926

7

Special Advice
for Girls

MAKE SURE YOUR BLOOMERS MATCH YOUR DRESS. Older girls' bloomers are not supposed to show—they're usually black or some dark color. Younger girls' frocks are so short that their bloomers stick out underneath. Don't be caught with bloomers that clash with your dress! Tuck a handkerchief under your bloomer elastic. Paper tissues have been invented, but they haven't caught on yet.

Price, **$2.98** Each
38E9766—Flesh.
Women's High Grade Crepe de Chine Bloomers. Bottoms neatly finished with hemstitching and ribbon bows. Reinforced at waist and crotch which insures extra wear. Elastic at waist and knees. Sizes, small, medium and large. **State size.** Shipping weight,

WEAR A HAT. Ladies won't leave the house without a hat, and most girls wear hats even to school. The most popular style, the cloche (pronounced *klōshe*), dips down so far in front that you can hardly see where you're going! It feels odd at first, but if you don't wear a hat, you may have to wear a huge bow that perches on top of your head like a butterfly. (Advice: Go with the hat.)

$1.98
78R6520

$1.59
78R6532

$1.48
78R654

104 10A SEARS, ROEBUCK AND CO.

TRY TO KEEP CLEAN. Your twenties mom may go crazy when your clothes get dirty—washing clothes in the twenties is even a bigger chore than washing people. You may be given aprons to put over your clothes after school, but both boys and girls will probably feel more comfortable in an old pair of knickers instead.

Keep up with the latest styles

Style is really important. You'll look swell and fit right in wearing these:

- patent leather shoes for dress
- a coat with a fur collar and cuffs
- a matching muff (for the matching-bloomer age)
- a pair of arctics: rubber boots that you pull over your shoes

Special Advice
for Boys

Twenties boys have a special sense of what's "darb." Here's how to fit in:

DRESS UP FOR TRAVEL OR SCHOOL. Button a clean collar and a clean pair of cuffs on your shirt. Next, put on your tie—you'll wear one every day except Saturday. Top everything off with knickers and a shawl-collared sweater or a jacket.

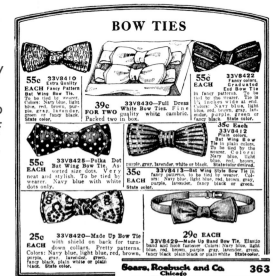

WEAR SUSPENDERS. Belts are only for church or fancy parties.

CARRY A NEEDLE AND THREAD. You'll spend so much time on your knees playing marbles that you'll wear holes in your knickers. To prevent this, some moms insist that boys wear their knickers above their knees, which is embarrassing. Instead, do a quick patch-up job before you get home. But be careful not to sew your pants to your union suit!

ALWAYS WEAR A GOLF CAP. Golf and golf caps are in.

GET USED TO BUTTON FLIES. Although zippers have been invented, they're still not used much for clothes.

How to Walk

The popular walking sound for boys is a loud *clack*. Soon after you arrive, take your high-tops to a shoe repair shop and get some metal heel plates nailed on. (Note the special high-top jackknife pocket.) Moms often insist on corduroy knickers because they don't easily wear out, but the noise the pant legs make when they rub is embarrassingly loud. Avoid making this sound by walking slightly bowlegged. Like this!

9

Being sick in the twenties is the pits. So take our advice:

TAKE SOME BAND-AIDS WITH YOU

Band-Aids are invented in 1921, but they are usually unavailable. It's hard to keep a cut free of infection without them, and there are no antibiotics in the twenties to cure one.

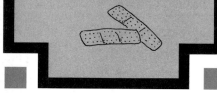

BEFORE YOU COME, GET YOUR SHOTS.

There are few inoculations and modern medicines available in the twenties, so whooping cough, typhus, scarlet fever, polio, mumps, measles, chicken pox, and flu are common and can be dangerous. If you get any of these, your house may be quarantined—no one will be allowed in or out until you are well!

WILLIAMS' ANTI~PAHN OINTMENT W-A-P-O

A TWENTIES FIRST

First Kleenex 1924

First Band-Aid 1921

COME BACK HOME FOR MODERN MEDICAL ATTENTION!

If something like a cut or a sore throat doesn't heal quickly, you might have an infection. This can be serious in the twenties, without antibiotics to fight it.

If you need a doctor, you'll want to come home to modern medicine. The twenties doctor, who comes to your bedside with a barn-shaped black leather bag full of syringes and smelly bottles, may lack the scientific know-how or prescription drugs to cure you.

MONEY

IT'S TIME TO CHECK OUT YOUR TRAVEL ALLOWANCE. Most twenties kids don't have much money—a quarter a week is considered a generous allowance. But your trunk contains a whopping ten "smackeroos" for each week of travel! You're not impressed? Wait until you see what a twenties dollar buys—you're going to go absolutely wild, trying to decide how to spend it all! Movies cost a dime, sometimes a quarter, ice cream cones a nickel, and five-and-ten-cent stores are full of things that really do cost five and ten cents.

FUNNY MONEY. Twenties money will look funny to you—you'll see buffaloes on nickels and the Statue of Liberty on dimes, and much bigger paper bills than you're used to. Bills were quite large until 1929, when they were made smaller—the size you're used to—to cut production costs.

WHAT ONE DOLLAR WILL BUY IN THE TWENTIES

Ten streetcar rides

One pair clamp-on hockey skates

Ten movie tickets

20 candy bars

Two haircuts

One short airplane ride

One 13-inch Little Orphan Annie doll

One baby doll that says "Mama"

One 10-inch talking teddy bear

20 ice cream cones

Two hardcover children's adventure novels

One professional league baseball

TWENTIES BOOMS...

Now that you've checked out your travel allowance, here are a few words of caution about spending money in the twenties. President Calvin Coolidge, elected in 1924, proclaims that "the chief business of the American people is business." The economy really booms. Many people have money and they are spending it. The more adventurous are buying exciting new conveniences— refrigerators, sewing machines, electric irons, washing machines, better cars, canned foods. But be careful—things are not quite what they seem.

WATCH OUT FOR FALSE ADVERTISING! Advertising is so new in the twenties that there are no laws against making extravagant claims for a product. Not all ads make false promises, but some do. Magazine ads are beginning to appear in color, too, and who can resist that?

AVOID BUYING ANYTHING ON CREDIT. For the first time, people can buy things without paying all at once—they can pay over time, in installments. By 1929, credit buying has increased five times over 1920 credit purchases! Don't do it—the economy is not as strong as it seems!

...AND BUSTS!

In 1928, Herbert Hoover is elected president, promising everyone "two chickens in every pot and a car in every garage." But President Hoover is wrong—by the end of 1929, the boom busts!

GET OUT OF THE TWENTIES BEFORE OCTOBER 29, 1929! This is the day of the famous New York stock market crash! On this day and the days following, many banks close, businesses go bankrupt, and stores and factories shut down. Millions of people—rich and poor—lose everything they own. Many lose their jobs.

This is the beginning of the Great Depression of the 1930s, known as "Hard Times." It's no place for a holiday. Many a family that was well off in the twenties (even yours) will endure poverty and hardship for years to come. But don't worry —you can escape on the Time Line before it happens!

FPG INTERNATIONAL

DON'T WARN ANYONE!

You'll want to warn your twenties family and friends about the coming crash, but no one will believe you. People are sure that the good times will only get better. Eventually they do, but "Hard Times" and the Second World War come first.

shhh...

13

TIME TRAVEL

1920

* Women vote for the first time.
* First scheduled radio program is broadcast.
* Dresses lose their waistlines.
* New word: *sundae*.

Ticket, Please!

Now that you're packed, dressed, and in the know, it's time to ride the Time Line! When you're choosing your seat, remember that you are going to be riding backward through time! All aboard!

1990 ➡ 1980 ➡ 1970 ➡ 1960 ➡ 1950 ➡ 1940 ➡ 1930 ➡

Here we are, pulling into the twenties! Choose any local station—your ticket may be used as many times as you wish—but don't miss these sights as we pass by.

1921

* Warren Harding becomes president.
* Almost one-quarter of all Americans are under the age of ten!
* Albert Einstein wins the Nobel Prize.
* First Miss America Contest is held.

1922

* First woman senator, Rebecca L. Fenton of Georgia, takes office.
* King Tutankhamen's tomb is discovered, revealing a mummy and fabulous treasures.
* First skywriting appears.
* Bobbed hair becomes the rage.
* Charles Atlas becomes a famous muscle man.

1923

* President Harding dies. Calvin Coolidge becomes President.
* Rin Tin Tin becomes the world's most famous dog, a movie star!
* Hollywood sign is erected over Hollywood, California.

14

1929

★ New York stock market crashes, sending panic throughout the nation.

★ Al Capone guns down enemies in Valentine's Day massacre.

★ Paper money is made smaller.

★ Babe Ruth hits his five hundredth home run.

1928

★ Amelia Earhart is the first woman to fly across the Atlantic Ocean.

★ First Academy Award ceremonies are held.

★ Alexander Fleming discovers penicillin.

★ First Mickey Mouse cartoon, *Steamboat Willie*, is shown.

1927

★ Charles Lindbergh flies nonstop from New York to Paris.

★ Harlem Globetrotters become the first Black American basketball team.

★ Babe Ruth hits sixty home runs in one season.

★ First cyclone roller coaster is built on Coney Island, New York.

1924

★ Lenin dies in Russia.

★ Native Americans are made citizens by Congress.

★ First *Little Orphan Annie* comic strip appears.

★ Everyone's dancing the Charleston!

1925

★ Charles Rogers flies the first nonstop flight from San Francisco to Honolulu.

★ First woman governor, Nellie Tayloe Ross, is elected in Wyoming.

★ Ku Klux Klan marches on Washington.

★ An all-electric radio is invented. ♪

★ Cars come in colors, not just black.

1926

★ Gangster Al Capone runs the mob in Chicago.

★ Gertrude Ederle is the first woman to swim the English Channel.

★ Magician Harry Houdini stays underwater for ninety-one minutes with only six minutes of air!

★ Skirts are the shortest yet in American history.

ARRIVAL

Welcome to the twenties! A Model T Ford with a special Time Line driver is waiting to take you wherever you wish. We suggest that your first stop be the beauty parlor (for girls) or the barbershop (for boys). On your way there, take a look at your new twenties downtown!

Nicknames

Look at all those black cars! Most of them are Model T Fords—until the later twenties, half the cars on the road are Model T's. (In 1927, the last year it was produced, the Model T cost $290.) Twenties folks give nicknames to things and people they especially like, so they call the Model T's "Tin Lizzies." Some nicknames twenties kids use for one another are "Owl," "Stilt," "Slats," "Dutch," "Spider," "Curly," "Red," and "Babs." Why not think up one for yourself!

JIVE TALK

Now's a good time to unpack your Jive Talk Twenties Dictionary. You can brush up while you're waiting your turn to get your new haircut. Twenties kids think slang is "the bee's knees." Soon you won't take any "guff" from anyone! Get started on the right "dog," and play around with a few of these "jake" words and expressions:

all righty	okay
amusing	terrific
baloney	nonsense
banana oil	nonsense
the berries	just great
bob	short haircut
buck	dollar
buffalo	nickel
bunk	nonsense
cheaters	eyeglasses
darb	with it
digs	home
divine	just wonderful
dog	foot
feller	boy or man
flapper	stylish young woman
flat tire	boring person
goofy	silly
guff	back talk
half-pint	small kid
hep	with it

het up	angry
high jinks	mischievous playfulness
hooch	alcoholic beverage
horsefeathers	nonsense
hotsy totsy	fancy
jake	with it
jalopy	beat-up old car
jive	jazz
keen	great
kisser	mouth
little shavers	kids smaller than you
lollygagging	being lazy
lounge lizard	playboy
mob	gangsters
peeved off	angry
razz	tease
razzle-dazzle	fancy stuff
ritzy	posh
sheik	stylish young man

smacker	dollar
smackeroo	dollar
smeller	nose
spiffy	dressed up
super	terrific
swell	terrific
swank	fancy
two bits	25 cents

a swank feller

You look like a spiffy sheik!

YOU'RE THE PIG'S WINGS, DARLING!

Believe it or not, it's a compliment if someone tells you you look like one of these:

✔ the eel's ankles

✔ the snake's hips

✔ the bee's knees

✔ the clam's garters

✔ the cat's meow

✔ the tiger's spots

It's "hep" to make up your own: "You look like the lion's lips! The ant's pants! The leopard's stripes!"

THE BEAUTY PARLOR

You'll need a twenties hairdo or you'll be found out in no time, so stop in a beauty parlor for your complimentary twenties styling. Here are some hair do's and don'ts:

CURLY HAIR IS IN, BUT *DON'T* GET A PERMANENT. The strong smell that hits you when you enter the beauty parlor comes from the permanent wave machine dangling from the ceiling. This monster is dangerous! The operator rolls sections of hair onto rollers, using a smelly curling solution. Then she attaches one of the tubes to each roller. When the electricity is turned on, steam shoots down the tubes. The stench is awful, and the steam can burn your scalp!

***DO* GET YOUR HAIR BOBBED (CUT SHORT).** Get a Dutch cut or a King Tut cut, haircuts that fit neatly under the popular twenties head-hugging hats. If you want to keep your hair long, have it twisted up in rags to make ringlets, which you can tie back with hair ribbons.

A TWENTIES FIRST

First permanent wave

1924

***DO* USE HAIR RIBBONS.** Hair ribbons are in, even for short hair. Get wide ones in lots of colors for just pennies at any five-and-ten-cent store.

THE BARBERSHOP

To find the barbershop, just look for a twirling red-and-white pole. The barbershop stinks, too, but here the problem is cigar smoke! Many twenties men smoke cigars or chew tobacco. The big metal bowls on the floor are *spittoons* for tobacco chewers to spit in. While you wait, start getting your twenties bearings by listening in on the many conversations, or study your Jive Talk Twenties Dictionary.

EXPECT THE BARBER TO BE HORRIFIED AT YOUR HAIR— it's probably too long or too short or too *something*. He'll be in a hurry to correct this. Let him. He'll plop you in a huge barber chair, wrap you up in a sheet, and attack the front of your hair with a comb and scissors. Next he'll take hand clippers to the sides. Last he'll shave your neck with a dangerous-looking straightedge razor and slap on some stinging linament. Ouch! The price? "Two bits" (twenty-five cents), and don't you look darb!

Where do you want to go next? Why, to your twenties home, of course.

21

HOME, SWEET HOME!

Welcome to your middle-class home in a middle-size city in middle America. Say "Hello, ma'am" and "How do you do, sir" to your twenties mom and dad, which is how polite kids in the twenties often address their parents. Here is some first-day savvy:

BE SURE TO ARRIVE HUNGRY! You will be treated to a big welcome dinner and urged to eat more mashed potatoes, more gravy, more roast beef, and more homemade rolls (no salad). Everything is made deliciously from scratch! Store-bought canned foods, although available, are rarely used, and there's no freezer in the house, so forget frozen foods. But be sure to leave room for the homemade desserts—like sailor's duff, charlotte russe, or chocolate cake. It's worth a trip to the twenties just to taste them.

PLAN TO ARRIVE ON A SATURDAY. Saturday is baking day, when you can enjoy bread, cookies, and cake warm from the oven. Plastic wrap and bags are unknown—bread is stored unwrapped in a tin bread box—so it doesn't stay fresh for long!

TURN ON THE HOT WATER. Saturday is also bath night. If this sounds disagreeable to you, take heart: *This may be the only bath you'll get all week!* Hot water does not just run out of the tap, so after dinner, watch your twenties dad light the gas fire in the hot water heater in the basement. The water will take about an hour to heat up. Then it will run out of a special tap on the upstairs tub.

WASH YOUR HAIR IN THE KITCHEN SINK. While you're waiting for your bathwater, bring in a potful

of rainwater from the barrel in the backyard and heat that up on the stove (your mom will have to light it for you). Shampoo your hair in the kitchen sink with Packer's tar soap shampoo.

TRY TO BE FIRST IN THE BATH. Two people often use the same bathwater, because the water heater heats only enough for one tubful. Twenties people don't like to waste anything, not even bathwater. Hurry, though, so the water won't be cold for the next "feller."

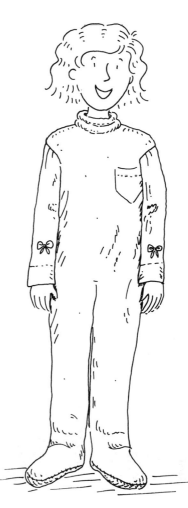

DON'T MENTION PAJAMAS! If it's winter, you'll want to hurry into your Dr. Dentons—a giant wool sleeper with *feet!* It itches, and you'll feel silly in it, but it's warm. Your twenties house can really get cold at night, especially since the furnace's coal fire often goes out. If it's summer, girls wear nightgowns and boys wear nightshirts. Pajamas are the latest rage, but don't risk asking for them— some families still think they're indecent.

SMELL THE SHEETS. When you finally fall into bed, be sure to smell the sunshine. Your sheets were dried in it outside on a clothesline!

23

AROUND THE HOUSE

Here are some house rules to help you learn your way around your twenties home:

RECYCLE! If you don't want to keep hearing "Waste not, want not" from your twenties parents, think twice before you throw anything out. Add string to the roll in the kitchen drawer, save newspapers to help start the fire in the stove, and save worn-out clothing for quilts and rags.

Although your twenties parents never heard of recycling, they probably do it better than most people you know in your own time.

USE ELECTRIC LIGHTS ONLY WHEN ABSOLUTELY NECESSARY. Most families find the fairly new electric light bills so shocking that a light left on really upsets them. To turn a light out, push in the bottom, dark-colored button. To turn it back on, push the top, light-colored button.

USE THE TELEPHONE SPARINGLY. Although most people have a telephone, kids are not encouraged to use it. If you can walk to visit a friend, you will. Long-distance calls are made only in real emergencies or on special occasions.

WHO'S WIRED?

By the middle twenties, only half of American homes are wired for electricity. Most of those use their new power source mostly for lights.

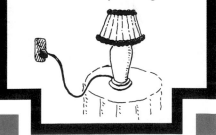

DON'T LOOK FOR SEVEN-DIGIT PHONE NUMBERS! There are fewer people in the twenties, and many of them still don't have telephones—in 1920, more than 85 percent of Americans are without one—so telephone numbers need only three to five digits.

YOU CAN'T CALL JUST ANYBODY. Some twenties towns, like yours, have two telephone companies. You can talk only to people who are on your system. If you're on Bell, you can't call anybody on Citizen's!

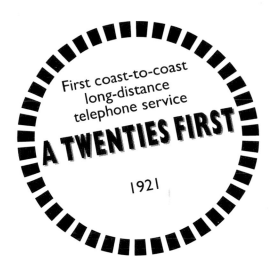

First coast-to-coast long-distance telephone service

A TWENTIES FIRST

1921

HOW TO USE THE TELEPHONE

You've noticed that your twenties phone has no dial or buttons? No problem. If it's a heavy black desk telephone, lift off the earpiece, put it against your ear, and wait for the operator to come on. Talk into the mouthpiece on top of the base, give the operator the number you're calling—435, for example—and she'll connect you. If your family has a wall telephone, stand on a chair to talk into the mouthpiece.

BREAKFAST

Some things don't change—twenties moms believe in a good breakfast, too, like bacon and pancakes, or french toast and hot cocoa, or cereal and milk.

BE SURE TO SHAKE THE MILK BOTTLE BEFORE YOU POUR. Milk is not homogenized—you can actually see the cream that rises to the top quarter of the glass bottle. Keep one hand over the top before you shake it, or the paper cap might fly off—and a mighty spray of milk with it!

TRY NOT TO SPILL. There are no paper towels or plastic sponges to quick-fix a twenties mess. To clean up, you'll need to fill a pail with water, shave some soap off a big bar with a knife if there is no powdered soap, wipe things up with a heavy string mop, then refill the pail to rinse.

KEEP A SHARP EYE ON THE TOASTER. To make toast, slice two pieces of homemade bread. Lean them, tentlike, on the toaster. When the first side is done, turn the toast, watch it, and then take it out before it burns. Spread on real butter — no margarine here — and homemade jam.

Breakfast Cereal Choices

Quaker oatmeal, Kellogg's corn flakes, and All-Bran are available throughout the twenties, but you can't get Wheaties until 1924 or Rice Krispies or shredded wheat until 1928. Sugar-coated cereals? Not a chance!

SWALLOW A SPOONFUL OF COD LIVER OIL!

Your twenties mom will insist. It tastes awful, but there aren't any vitamin pills yet, and you really don't want to get a cold, because there aren't any cold medications either!

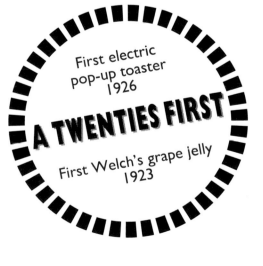

First electric
pop-up toaster
1926

A TWENTIES FIRST

First Welch's grape jelly
1923

Like twenties kids, you can't play until your chores are done. You might even enjoy them!

EMPTY THE ICE PAN (DAILY). Food in the icebox on the back porch is kept cold with real ice brought by the iceman. The huge ice block on top melts and dribbles into a pan at the bottom. Pull out the pan and dump the water in the yard. If you forget, it will overflow and you'll be the one who will have to mop up the floor!

STOKE THE FURNACE (DAILY, IN WINTER). The house is heated with a coal-burning furnace in the basement, and somebody has to keep the fire going. To stoke the furnace, pull out the ash pan and empty the ashes into a big ash bin. Empty the "clinkers" (pieces that didn't burn). Then shovel some coal from the coal room into the furnace door. Caution: this is guaranteed to make you dirty!

BEAT THE RUGS (ONCE IN A WHILE). Electric vacuum cleaners, although available, are still not found in most homes. So on a serious cleaning day, you'll be asked to help hang rugs over a clothesline in the backyard and beat the dust out of them with a bamboo rug beater. Do this on a Saturday—you'll be itching for a bath!

HELP WITH THE WASH (MONDAYS). For each load (there are sure to be four or five), your mom pours hot water into an electric washing machine, shaves some soap in from a big brown bar, and turns on the machine: *Rou-oomp-oomp, rou-oomp-oomp, rou-oomp-oomp.* After a while, she drains out the water, cranks the steaming clothes through the wringer, rinses them, and cranks them through again. Your job is hauling the heavy wet clothes to the backyard to hang up on clotheslines with wooden clothespins.

TAKE IN THE WASH (MONDAYS). The laundry is a good deal lighter than it was this morning, and the big baskets smell outdoor-fresh!

WIND THE CLOCKS. Electric and battery-powered clocks are still rare. Most twenties clocks are spring-powered, eight-day clocks. One wind up keeps them going for eight days.

RUN ERRANDS. Your twenties dad probably takes the only family car to work, so if your mom needs anything, you'll be sent to get it. This is fun!

At the **meat market,** watch the butcher cut your order right off the carcass with a huge saw or knife. For a few cents, fish a big dill from the pickle barrel.

Don't miss a cookie from the cookie rack at the **grocery store.**

If there's to be ice cream for dessert, you'll have to run and get a quart from the corner **drugstore** after supper: Your choices are vanilla, chocolate, or strawberry. With no freezer at home, you'll have a good excuse to eat it all!

DELIVERIES

Exploring your twenties town starts at your own front—and back—doors! Since most twenties moms don't have a car for shopping, almost everything comes to the house.

MILK is delivered every morning in glass quarts (no half-gallons or gallons).

ICE arrives every other day. The iceman clamps a twenty-five-pound block in giant tongs and carries it on his back to the icebox on the back porch. (While he's busy, sneak in the truck for slivers of ice to suck on.)

GROCERIES arrive in big baskets (no grocery bags yet) after your mom phones in her order. Check for a chocolate bar or some peppermints—it's not uncommon for the grocer to throw in some for free if your mom is a steady customer.

COAL is delivered in huge baskets and dumped down a chute in a basement window. Although there aren't many horse-pulled vehicles in the twenties—even the fire engines are gas-powered now—sometimes horses do pull the coal wagons, so watch for them.

GARBAGE is carried from the house in big cans and dumped into a truck (paper trash is usually burned in the stove). The whole smelly heap goes to the city piggery, where the hogs eat it. It's one way some twenties towns recycle their garbage.

SURPRISE! There are **brushes, men's suits, buttons, and goodness knows what else** at the door. Door-to-door salespeople are common. Kids sell things, too — like Scripto ink, dandelion greens, and the latest issue of the *Saturday Evening Post.* (If you want extra money, try it.)

PEDDLERS

Look for portable shops driven (or pulled by horses) slowly up and down the street. You may find some of these:

Fish man

Cheese man

Scissors grinder: Get your family's knives and scissors sharpened.

Fruit and vegetable man: Ask for a banana off the huge stalk on the back.

Ragman: He'll pay you a penny a pound for old newspapers.

Newsboy: Buy a paper to find out what's happening — radio is still not a common source of news, and there's no TV!

GETTING AROUND TOWN

STREETCAR SAVVY

Pay the fare. Get on at the front door and drop ten cents in the glass box next to the motorman's seat. Watch the money disappear when the motorman flips a lever. After he turns a crank, you can hear the coins being sorted—*tinka-tinka-tinka.*

Sit near the front. You can watch the motorman operate the car as you clack, bump, and clang down the middle of the street.

If it's crowded, give your seat to an older person. If you don't, everyone will glare at you and remark on how rude you are.

When you want to get off, pull the cord that runs near the ceiling. The motorman will stop at the next corner so you can step out the back door.

Twenties kids wouldn't dare ask a parent to chauffeur them around, and bicycles are used mostly by kids in high school or older, but don't despair! In most towns, streetcars run on tracks set into the street, powered by an overhead electric wire. For a dime, they'll take you almost anywhere.

Look for a Souvenir

While you're out and about, keep your eyes peeled for a swell souvenir to take home with you. You can have anything you can pay for with your allowance.

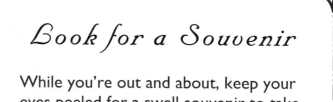

PEOPLE WATCHING

While riding the streetcar, look for two of the most interesting kinds of people you're apt to see anywhere: flappers and sheiks! Flappers (sometimes called "shebas") are young twenties women with a special kind of sass. They're often seen with dashing young men dressed "to the nines," called sheiks. These are the rebellious young men and women of the twenties— they listen to jazz, dance the Charleston, party, and sing. No one carries the twenties high spirits with more style.

THE MOVIES

Know Some Stars

Twenties kids are always talking about their favorite movie stars. Drop a few of these names and you'll fit right in: **Rin Tin Tin**, the Wonder Dog; slapstick artists **Laurel and Hardy**; and **Charlie Chaplin**, the most loved comedian of all time. **Rudolph Valentino**, star of *The Sheik*, is a romantic hero. And there isn't a more glamorous heroine than **Mary Pickford**. There are many more. After you see a **Tom Mix** western, you can play "Tom Mix" with your friends (all twenties kids love pretending to be cowboys).

Now that you're out and about, why not go to a show? Not much gets you more for a dime or a quarter than Saturday at the movies! A twenties theater alone is worth the price of admission. It's called a "movie palace"—and it is, with a big stage, velvet curtains, and fancy decorations!

Laurel and Hardy

IF YOU WANT A "TALKIE," WAIT UNTIL 1927.
Before 1927, all movies are silent—no sound tracks at all. When the actors speak, the words flash on the screen. A piano player on stage plays the background music.

CATCH A CLIFF-HANGER. Cartoons starring such comic characters as the Katzenjammer Kids or Felix the Cat are followed by previews and advertisements. Then comes the first movie. If you're lucky, the second movie will be one of a series, with a chilling, cliff-hanging ending that stops at the most exciting part. Come back next week to see what happens! (All the movies will be black-and-white.)

Mary Pickford

THE BETTMANN ARCHIVE

Charlie Chaplin

FPG INTERNATIONAL

First Mickey
Mouse cartoon

A TWENTIES FIRST

1928

Tom Mix

THE BETTMANN ARCHIVE

WHERE TO GET ICE CREAM

Ice cream is a favorite twenties treat. You can buy it in quarts at the drugstore or in cones at the soda fountain, or even better . . .

Make it at home. Your twenties family probably churns ice cream at home in a big wooden bucket. You can help by taking a turn at the crank. It's a lot of work, but it's bound to be the best you ever tasted!

Find an ice cream parlor. These can be simple or very elaborate, but most have delicate, uncomfortable chairs with round wooden seats and curved metal backs. Ice cream parlors are a little more "swank" than your everyday drugstore, a nice place to take a friend.

After the movies, you might drop by the drugstore. Almost every twenties drugstore has a "soda fountain," a counter with rotating stools, where you can order a Coca-Cola, an ice cream cone, or the latest rage, an ice cream sundae! (Cones and Cokes, 5¢ each.)

BUY A MAGAZINE. While you're at the drugstore, pick up a magazine. Boys especially like boxing magazines, which they hoard, arguing about which champion is best. They're also impressed with *Whizbang,* a magazine thought to be racy (better hide that one under your bed!). Girls like to cut out the paper dolls, like Betsy McCall or Peter Pan, featured in the monthly *McCall's* magazine.

First Eskimo Pie (chocolate-covered ice cream bar)

A TWENTIES FIRST

1921

THE CANDY STORE

Twenties kids usually don't have much spending money. What's left after movies and ice cream is usually spent at the candy store. Give yourself some time to study the large display in the front window. Here's what you'll find:

First
Wrigley's
chewing gum

A TWENTIES FIRST

1921

PENNY CANDY

- ◆ licorice sticks (red or black)
- ◆ wax elephants with sweet liquid inside
- ◆ lollipops with rope handles
- ◆ Tootsie Rolls
- ◆ big flat taffy bars
- ◆ jawbreakers

5¢ CANDY

- ◆ Mars bars
- ◆ Milky Way bars
- ◆ Hershey bars
- ◆ Wrigley's chewing gum
- ◆ Bloodberry gum
- ◆ Mounds bars
- ◆ Butterfingers
- ◆ Dubble Bubble

5¢ ICE CREAM TREATS

Look in the freezer for Popsicles, Eskimo Pies, and ice cream bars. Check the stick of your ice cream bar—if it says *FREE*, you get another one!

37

SPORTS HEROES

Before you go to school, you'll want to brush up on the sports heroes that everyone there will be talking about. If you're in Cleveland on August 11, 1929, be sure to go see Yankee slugger Babe Ruth hit his five hundredth home run! Whoever catches that ball gets a new ball autographed by the "King of Swat" himself and twenty dollars!

FPG INTERNATIONAL

Babe Ruth

BASEBALL

Babe Ruth (George Herman Ruth) hits fifty four home runs in one season for the New York Yankees in 1920, and sixty in 1927. And in 1929, he hits his five hundredth home run!

HORSE RACING

Man O'War ("Big Red") sets five American speed records. (1920)

BASKETBALL

The original **Celtics** start getting popular (1923). The **Harlem Globetrotters** are organized (1927).

SWIMMING

Johnny Weissmuller sets a record, swimming 200 yards freestyle in 1 minute $59\frac{1}{2}$ seconds (1923).

GOLF

Bobby Jones becomes a golf hero (1925). Twenties kids are crazy about golf, even though they rarely play the game. The women's golf hero, champion six times, is the great athlete Glenna Colett.

UPI/BETTMANN

Man O'War

38

TENNIS

Helen Wills and **Bill Tilden** win the U.S. Open singles (1923).

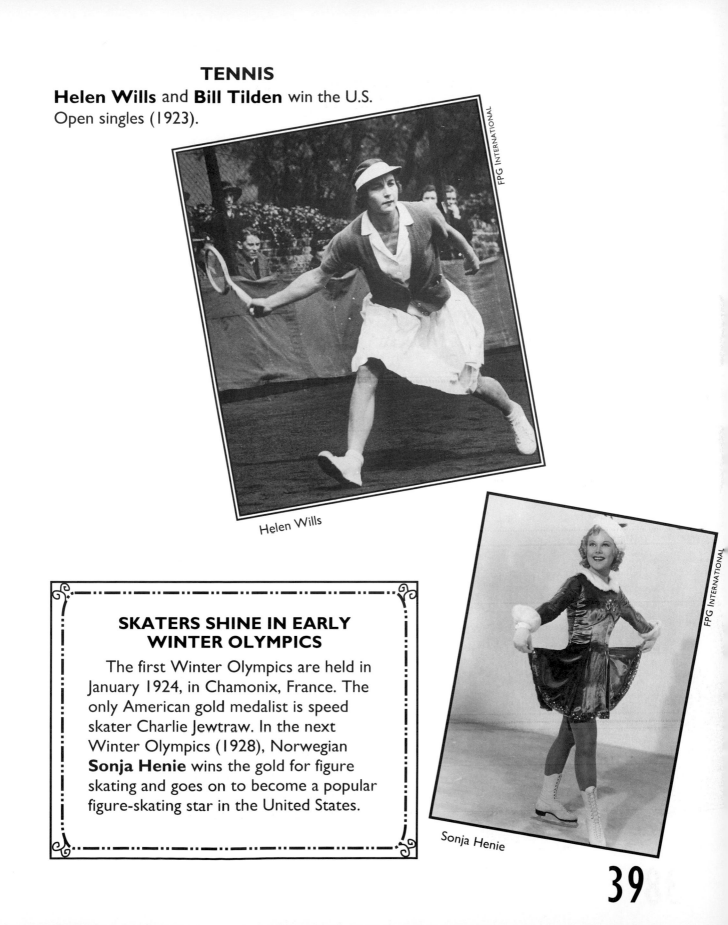

Helen Wills

SKATERS SHINE IN EARLY WINTER OLYMPICS

The first Winter Olympics are held in January 1924, in Chamonix, France. The only American gold medalist is speed skater Charlie Jewtraw. In the next Winter Olympics (1928), Norwegian **Sonja Henie** wins the gold for figure skating and goes on to become a popular figure-skating star in the United States.

Sonja Henie

39

First Scotch tape

A TWENTIES FIRST

1928

New laws in the twenties require all children to go to school, so we suggest you get there before you are picked up by a truant officer for "vagrancy" (hanging around) or "playing hooky" (skipping school). Look for a big brick building with a gravel playground. You'll smell the oiled wooden floors when you go in.

Your subjects will sound familiar—reading, writing, arithmetic, spelling, grammar, history, and science—but the textbooks have no color pictures, and the print is small. Your desk is either nailed to the floor or attached to the desks in front of and in back of you. Check these out, too:

A TWENTIES SCHOOL DICTIONARY

☞ **Culture points**   Extra credit points. Earn these by visiting the library or the museum or by taking music lessons.

☞ **Deportment**   Behavior. Better "mind your p's and q's." You will be graded on this.

☞ **Elocution**   Public speaking. You will be required to memorize poems and recite them in front of the whole class.

☞ **Inkwell**   The pot of dark liquid in your desk.

☞ **Nib**   A pen point. Stick one in a pen handle, dip it in the inkwell, and write. (This takes practice, but there are no ballpoint pens.)

DON'T SHOW OFF! You know about computers, space flights, men on the moon, plastics, and events to come that your twenties teachers never heard of. Don't let on! You might blow your cover!

WATCH OUT FOR FINGERNAIL INSPECTIONS. Teachers may spring these on you unexpectedly!

CHILD LABOR LESSENS

Until, and even during, the twenties, it is not uncommon for children as young as five to ten years old to hold full-time jobs. By 1930, however, every state has passed laws requiring school attendance, tripling the number of consolidated schools in twelve years and helping to control the exploitation of children as cheap labor.

GAMES

After school, head for the playground. Boys have the advantage here—they get to wear rubber-and-canvas basketball high-tops, while girls skid around in their ankle-high leather shoes.

JOIN IN THE STATUE GAME. The person who is "it" stands at a home base and counts out loud. Whenever he or she stops counting and yells "Statues!" everyone has to freeze on the spot. The first person caught moving becomes it, and then the other players try to get back to the home base without being tagged by the new it. The first person tagged becomes it, and the game begins again.

PLAY SCRUB. When there's not enough players for baseball or softball, play Scrub. When a batter is struck out, everyone changes places — the catcher moves to the bat, the pitcher moves to catcher, the first-base player moves to pitcher, and so on. (Hint: It's considered bad manners to quit before everyone has had a chance at bat.)

MARBLES FOR BOYS

Twenties boys spend a lot of time on their knees playing marbles. Buy some "glassies" (transparent marbles), "agates" (white with colored swirls), and "Donnecks" (big ones), and join right in. Prepare to lose a few, but if you get good enough, you just might win them back!

A TWENTIES FIRST

First pogo stick 1920

First frog-jumping jubilee 1928

TWENTIES GIRLS JUMP ROPE FOR HOURS. You can skip by yourself, but it's more fun when others turn a long rope while you jump. Soon you'll be jumping "double Dutch"— between two ropes turning in opposite directions. There are lots of jumping rhymes, but they often end in double-quick time, called "peppers," sometimes preceded by "Seeder, cider, red-hot pepper!" Jacks are popular, too, so be sure to buy some with your allowance.

DON'T PASS THE FOOTBALL!

There are many football games, like Association, in which one team tries to kick the ball over the goal line more times than the other team. Whatever game you play, don't pass the football. For most of the twenties, footballs are for kicking, not throwing! Knute Rockne, Notre Dame's famous football coach, has only recently introduced the forward pass. The twenties football is huge and round, and the ends aren't as pointed as you're used to, so it's easier to kick.

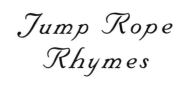

Jump Rope Rhymes

Practice jumping rope to these, and you'll be one of the twenties crowd in no time:

Cinderella, dressed in yella,
Went downtown to buy some jella.
On her way her girdle busted.
How many people were disgusted?
1, 2, 3, 4 . . . (Peppers: Count until you miss a jump.)

Apples, peaches, pears, and plums.
Tell me when your birthday comes.
(Peppers: Chant the months until your birthday, then the days until your birthday—if you can!)

DON'T LOSE YOUR SKATE KEY!

Everybody roller-skates, but twenties skates are made of metal and don't have shoes attached. Tighten them on your shoes with a skate key and then keep the key on a string around your neck!

43

LOOK FOR SOME OF YOUR FAVORITES!

These new twenties books will stay popular for more than fifty years!

Doctor Doolittle, by Hugh Lofting

The Velveteen Rabbit, by Margery Williams

Winnie-the-Pooh, by A. A. Milne

Bambi, by Felix Salten

No TV—So Read!

The great radio programs for kids don't get going until the thirties. But there is an alternative to the radio's classical music, jazz, church broadcasts, farm news, and stock market reports: books! Kids' books in the twenties are exciting. Heroes and heroines travel, invent things, explore, solve crimes, fly in biplanes, and dangle over chasms. Series are especially popular, so if you like one book, you'll find more just like it.

RUTH FIELDING

Girls love the Ruth Fielding books, by Alice B. Ermicson. This heroine really gets around! Try these:

Ruth Fielding in the Far North

Ruth Fielding at Golden Pass

Ruth Fielding in Motion Pictures

TOM SWIFT

Boys especially love Tom Swift, a genius boy inventor. Here are a few of the many titles:

Tom Swift and His Air Glider

Tom Swift and His Wizard Camera

Tom Swift and His Electric Locomotive

44

First public demonstration of television

A TWENTIES FIRST

1928

The Sears, Roebuck Catalog

Most twenties kids can't afford to buy toys at the local department store. Instead, they have fun "window shopping" in the family's Sears, Roebuck catalog. You can, too—every family has one. Here are some twenties toys you might find there:

POWER TOYS. Twenties toys don't use batteries. Instead, most toys wind up for power. You can get nine- and ten-inch metal models of the latest twenties cars and trucks (25¢), and bigger models, too (47¢). There are even animal or circus wind-up toys that hop or jump or do circus tricks.

BABY DOLLS. It's a big deal if a doll says "Mama" or cries.

PAPER DOLLS. Most twenties girls collect paper dolls. Pool your collections and you'll have enough to play with for hours.

TEDDY BEARS. The ones with jointed head, arms, and legs are most popular in the twenties.

RIDING TOYS. Children's bicycles are still so new that most twenties kids don't have one. Don't worry. There are other riding toys: scooters ($2.89), red metal wagons ($5.98), and best of all, the Genuine Irish Mail ($9.95), which goes lickety-split when you pump the handle.

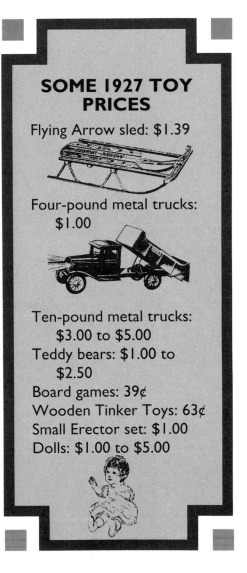

SOME 1927 TOY PRICES

Flying Arrow sled: $1.39

Four-pound metal trucks: $1.00

Ten-pound metal trucks: $3.00 to $5.00
Teddy bears: $1.00 to $2.50
Board games: 39¢
Wooden Tinker Toys: 63¢
Small Erector set: $1.00
Dolls: $1.00 to $5.00

Can't find the catalog? Look in the bathroom! Some families use the catalog pages for toilet paper!

Even without TV, twenties kids are rarely bored. Here are some other things they do to amuse themselves. Try some!

COLLECT SOMETHING!

Join the fad mania by starting a collection! Twenties folks don't throw much away, and some things, like shiny foil gum and candy wrappers, are still new enough to seem amazing and valuable. Here are some other things you might try collecting:

string	pressed flowers
stamps	paper dolls
bottle caps	pictures cut from
marbles	magazines
postcards	baseball cards

GET A CRYSTAL SET!

A crystal set is a homemade radio that can tune in distant stations—sometimes as far away as five hundred or even a thousand miles. To get these stations, you have to string a whole lot of wire up on the roof for an antenna. You listen through a speaker that looks like a huge petunia, or better, through a pair of earphones so you don't annoy your twenties parents, who are used to a quiet house. To find a station, try to get the "cat's whisker" to hit the right part of the crystal. Now you can travel the airways. This will give you plenty to talk about with your friends, most of whom are vying to see who can tune in the most distant radio station.

FADS

There's always some new fad popping up in the twenties. You'll know what the latest one is—everybody will be talking about it. It might be one of these:

DANCE MARATHONS offer money prizes to the couple who can dance the longest. It could be days, or weeks! Other marathon events include kissing contests and roller-skating contests—you name it!

CROSSWORD PUZZLES are showing up in all the newspapers, and suddenly everybody's doing them. There are crossword puzzle contests, too.

OUIJA BOARDS. These gamelike boards are supposed to have special powers. The pointer "magically" indicates the answer to your questions.

FLAGPOLE SITTERS. Everybody's talking about Shipwreck Kelly, who started sitting on top of flagpoles in 1924. Some pole perchers stay up two weeks or more, and many of them are women.

IT'S A PLANE!

Whenever you hear an airplane, run outdoors and look up. Everybody does it. Planes were invented before the twenties, but they are new to the everyday sky.

FAMILY OUTINGS

Twenties families do lots of things together, especially on weekends and during summer vacations. Here are a few outings to look forward to.

DON'T MISS A TWENTIES PICNIC! Picnics are the main form of weekend entertainment for many families — church picnics, family picnics, company picnics, Boy Scout and Girl Scout picnics, and best of all, Fourth of July picnics. You'll be surprised at how the adults dress — women wear hats and wobble through the grass in high heels, while men play baseball in three-piece suits, starched collars, and straw hats. Kids can dress in knickers or other play clothes, though.

A TWENTIES FIRST

First helium-filled balloons 1921

First Hostess cakes 1927

Beach Tips

✔ **Swim *before* you eat.** Adults are sure you'll get cramps and drown if you don't wait a whole *hour* after you eat to swim.

✔ **Change into your "bathing costume" at the last minute.** The two-piece tank suit is 100 percent wool, and does it ever itch! (Everyone thinks twenties swim wear is *very* daring, though, so don't laugh.)

✔ **Put clothes *on* to go out in the sun.** Twenties folks are ahead of their time — they know the sun can be bad for your skin.

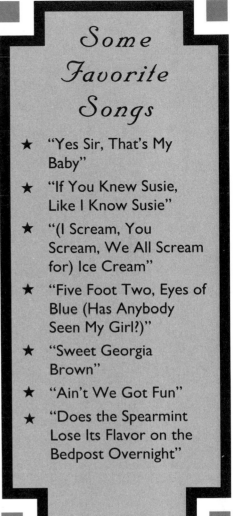

Some Favorite Songs

★ "Yes Sir, That's My Baby"

★ "If You Knew Susie, Like I Know Susie"

★ "(I Scream, You Scream, We All Scream for) Ice Cream"

★ "Five Foot Two, Eyes of Blue (Has Anybody Seen My Girl?)"

★ "Sweet Georgia Brown"

★ "Ain't We Got Fun"

★ "Does the Spearmint Lose Its Flavor on the Bedpost Overnight"

GO "OUT" FOR DINNER. Your twenties family almost never goes to restaurants, especially with kids. Their idea of eating out is more likely a big family dinner with aunts, uncles, cousins, probably at your grandparents' house. What a time! After a huge meal, you can enjoy listening to records or playing hide-and-seek outside. Later, join in singing hymns or popular songs around the piano. Family members who can play an instrument do, even if they sound terrible!

WITNESS A BARNSTORMING. Try to persuade your parents to drive you to the countryside to watch a barnstorming, an air show put on by a stunt pilot using a farmer's pasture for an airfield (which is how it got its name). Watch both men and women flying all kinds of amazing aerial stunts, as well as clowns performing daring stunts like wing walking and jumping from one plane to another. For five dollars (and with your parents' permission), you might even ride in an open-cockpit, two-seater biplane yourself!

49

AUTO TOURING

What You'll Do Without

You're not likely to find these in the twenties:

- ❑ Rearview mirrors
- ❑ Car heaters
- ❑ Reliable road maps
- ❑ Rest rooms at gas stations (Use the outhouse behind a school)
- ❑ Motels (Rent a little shack at an auto court)
- ❑ Car radios
- ❑ Superhighways and freeways
- ❑ Tollbooths
- ❑ Fast-food restaurants
- ❑ Bumper stickers

Your twenties family probably loves to travel, but you'll need a sense of adventure to go far on primitive twenties roads. Cars aren't equipped the way cars are today, road signs are scarce, and just try to find a readable map! You'll meet all sorts of interesting people as you ask directions, though. Just be prepared:

BRING AT LEAST *TWO* SPARE TIRES AND PLENTY OF SPARE PARTS. You will probably have several flat tires— twenties balloon tires aren't up to the terrible twenties roads—and you can count on one other serious breakdown as well.

PUT LOTS OF BLANKETS IN THE BACKSEAT. They will soften the bumpy ride, and you'll need them when you camp at night. There are almost no motels yet, and even most of the "auto courts" supply little more than a dry place for your bedroll. (Sorry, no sleeping bags yet, either.)

WEAR YOUR OLDEST CLOTHES. Many of the roads are only dirt or gravel, so you're bound to get dirty. You'll probably ride in an open car or in one with the windows open.

First car radio

A TWENTIES FIRST

1927

LONG-DISTANCE TRAVEL

The train is *the* twenties way to travel long distances. You can go almost anywhere on the train, anytime, even when winter roads are impassable for cars. You might even go to New York in time to see Lindbergh take off or to take part in a ticker tape parade!

ARRIVE AT THE STATION EARLY. You won't want to miss seeing the coal engine shooting huge clouds of steam from its stack when it arrives hissing, huffing, screeching, and clanging.

CHOOSE A SEAT BY THE WINDOW before the whistle blasts, the conductor shouts "All aboard!" and the train lurches forward. It's fun to wave back at the kids who wave to the train from the fences along the track.

EAT IN THE DINING CAR. Walk through the swaying cars to sit in the dining car and enjoy a fancy meal. You get white tablecloths, cloth napkins, and a real flower in a vase.

CHOOSE THE TOP BUNK. At night, the porter will turn your seat into a bed and lower another bed out of the ceiling to make bunk beds. Then he'll draw the heavy, red velvet curtains for privacy. If you dare, reach out and pat people's heads when they walk by!

51

TWENTIES WOMEN

First transport pilot's license granted to a woman

A TWENTIES FIRST

1927

Women vote for the first time!

Watch those twenties women . . .

- ☞ become active in sports, especially tennis, golf, skating, and swimming
- ☞ drive automobiles
- ☞ fly stunt planes, sit on flagpoles, and walk the wings of flying biplanes
- ☞ wear the shortest skirts ever seen before in America
- ☞ wear pants

Twenties women are demanding a more active role in life than they've ever had before. Just look at some of these feminine firsts:

1920

Women vote for the first time in American history.

1922

Sharpshooter Annie Oakley amazes everyone when she hits 98 out of 100 targets at the Pinehurst Gun Club in North Carolina.

Annie Oakley

UPI/BETTMANN NEWSPHOTOS

Gertrude Ederle

1924

Annie Jump Cannon, a recognized astronomer, has cataloged a quarter of a million stars! Nellie Tayloe Ross becomes the first woman to govern a state when she's elected governor of Wyoming.

1925

Dr. Florence Sabin, a nationally recognized medical researcher, is the first woman to be elected to the National Academy of Sciences.

1927

Phoebe Fairgrave Omlie is the first woman to receive a transport pilot's license.

1928

Anthropologist Margaret Mead publishes her first book, *Coming of Age in Samoa,* a study of people on a South Pacific island. Pilot Amelia Earhart becomes the first woman to fly across the Atlantic Ocean.

Amelia Earhart

Cheer "Our Trudy"

Help cheer Gertrude Ederle, nicknamed "Our Trudy" by her many fans. On August 6, 1926, heavily greased from head to toe, she becomes the first woman to swim the chilly English Channel. Gertrude Ederle is not only successful, but she also sets a record of 14 hours and 31 minutes, beating the men's record by two hours! At the end of her exhausting swim, welcoming British officials tell her she must hand over her passport before she can come ashore—all in fun, of course. When she returns to New York, she is welcomed by a huge ticker tape parade!

TWENTIES DISCRIMINATION

Time Line Travel guarantees the safety of all its tourists, but if you are a person of color or are Jewish, prepare for a good dose of twenties discrimination: racial slurs, put-downs, and segregated facilities of all kinds are common. Ku Klux Klan members slander, torture, and even murder many African-Americans, Catholics, Jews, Native Americans, Japanese-Americans, Chinese-Americans, and others. But twenties Americans of all colors and creeds are working for equality:

THE 1921 IMMIGRATION ACT. So many people are moving to America—about a million people a year—that many American-born citizens fear for their jobs and so are unfriendly to the newcomers. In the twenties, laws are passed to limit how many people can come into the United States every year.

1921

Albert Einstein, a German Jewish physicist, wins the Nobel Prize.

1924

Congress makes Native Americans citizens of the United States.

1926

New York publisher Alfred A. Knopf publishes *Weary Blues,* the first book of poetry by African-American poet Langston Hughes.

1927

The black Harlem Globetrotters basketball team, destined to become one of the most loved in America, is born.

1929

The Bessie Coleman Aero Clubs are organized to encourage aviation among African-Americans and to honor Bessie Coleman, a young daredevil stunt pilot, who in 1922 became the first licensed African-American woman aviator in the world.

Good news! In 1929, Martin Luther King, Jr., is born!

Martin Luther King, Jr.

" 'Taint Nobody's Business If I Do"

This song, sung by African-American blues artist Bessie Smith, is on the first jazz blues record, recorded in 1923. It makes quite a hit! It is part of the jazz and blues from the African-American community that changes the sound of American music.

LINDBERGH'S FAMOUS FLIGHT

3,600 miles ... 33½ hours

New York

LINDBERGH IS FLYING LIGHT!

Lindbergh takes only an inflatable raft, five sandwiches (he's afraid if he eats much, he'll fall asleep!), and a compass. He has no map, no radio, no parachute, and no heat!

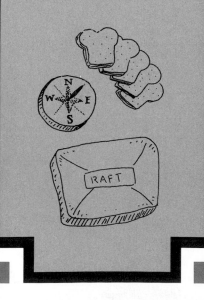

Be sure you don't miss the extraordinary excitement of Lindbergh's famous flight. Since 1920, a New York hotel owner has offered $25,000 to the first person to fly a plane nonstop across the Atlantic Ocean. Today, May 20, 1927, a twenty-five-year-old pilot with only four years' flying experience, who's never flown over water, is about to try. Not too big a crowd shows up at Roosevelt Field to watch him take off—many pilots have already tried and failed, and whoever heard of what's-his-name, anyway? You are there, though, because you are the only one who knows that Charles A. Lindbergh is about to become the twenties' most celebrated hero!

It is early morning. You watch Lindbergh climb into his one-engine plane. The wheels sink deep into the mud. He revs the engine and slogs slowly down the runway. Can he get going fast enough to take off? Few think he'll make it, but you're not worried. Just as It's about to hit the tractor at the end of the runway, the plane lifts suddenly, clearing the tractor by only fifteen feet! Charles Lindbergh and the *Spirit of St. Louis* are off on their famous 3,600-mile flight to Paris!

Over thirty-three hours later, Lindbergh approaches Paris. He's been spotted and the word's been radioed ahead! Rockets are exploding over the Paris airport, and cars line the runway with headlights blazing so Lindbergh can see to land! When his plane comes to a stop at 10:20 P.M., people swarm around his plane, cutting pieces of cloth off the wings for souvenirs and carrying "The Lone Eagle" on their shoulders. When his feet touch the ground a half an hour later, the first thing Lindbergh does is call his mother.

Charles A. Lindbergh

57

TICKER TAPE PARADES

Twenties New Yorkers are famous for celebrating their heroes and heroines with "ticker tape parades," which start at the waterfront and go to City Hall, where the honored person is welcomed by the mayor. Tons of confetti—often made from ticker tape, the long, narrow strips of paper on which stock market prices are continuously printed—flies from the windows of the buildings lining the street, falling on the crowds and into the many open automobiles. Noise roars joyfully. Be sure to join the surging crowds along the parade route. You can enjoy Charles Lindbergh's ticker tape parade on June 11, 1927, the biggest one of the decade.

A TWENTIES FIRST

First skywriting
1922

First parachuting
1922

LINDBERGH'S AMAZING WELCOME!

★ Four million people cheer at the New York parade

★ Eighteen hundred tons of paper is thrown

★ Lindbergh receives two million letters, 100,000 telegrams, and 14,000 presents

THE ROARING TWENTIES

You're nearing the end of your trip, but before you leave, be sure to take a peek at the "roaring" aspects of the twenties. Adults have found many ways to celebrate the good times after the long years of World War I (1914–1918). Watch twenties natives kick up their heels, but be careful— organized crime takes off in the twenties as well!

JAZZ IT UP! The Jazz Age is another twenties nickname. Jazz, introduced by black Americans, changes the beat of American music forever. Young people love its new, swinging sound and dance-inspiring beat. Listen to it on the radio, or play it on the gramophone.

How to Play the Gramophone

Wind up the crank and set the needle on the record, which plays at 78 rpm. The speaker is the horn. Notice how thick and heavy the records are.

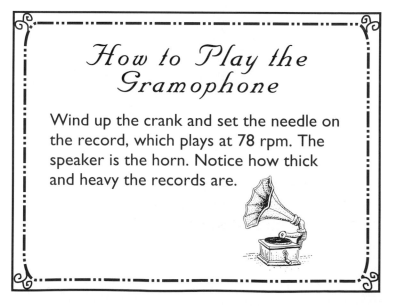

First electric jukebox
1927

A TWENTIES FIRST

First cyclone roller coaster
1927

DANCE THE CHARLESTON!

Unless you're in high school, you may not
be asked to a dance party, but learn how to do the
knock-kneed Charleston anyway—everybody's
doing it! This isn't called the Party Decade for
nothing!

PEEK INTO A SPEAKEASY, but better not go in! A speakeasy is a secret, illegal drinking club. To get in, you have to whisper a secret password through the hole in the door. Adults who want to drink sneak into speakeasies, but it's risky. Speakeasies are often busted by the police.

LOOK OUT FOR GANGSTERS. Groups of organized criminals—called "the mob"—make and smuggle illegal liquor. The most famous gang is in Chicago, run by Al Capone, but there are similar gangs all over the country. Gangsters war viciously with each other.

First White House Christmas tree lights

A TWENTIES FIRST

1923

The Age of Prohibition

In 1920, an amendment to the U.S. Constitution makes alcoholic beverages —beer, wine, and liquor—illegal for the entire country. The people of the Party Decade find ways to make, sell, and drink "hooch" anyway, all of them illegal. (The amendment will be repealed in 1933.)

TA-TA, TWENTIES!

Getting homesick? Now's a good time to leave—the stock market crash of 1929 is due any day now (October 29, 1929). But remember:

DON'T LEAVE WITHOUT GETTING YOUR PHOTOGRAPH TAKEN! The photographer will hide under a black cloth while he peers into one end of a big camera and you look into the other. Smile when he says, "Say 'Cheese!'"

DECIDE ON A SOUVENIR. Your ticket allows you to bring back one souvenir from the twenties. What will it be?

SEND A THANK-YOU LETTER TO YOUR TWENTIES FAMILY. Tell them what you liked best and when you plan to return. The stamp will cost two cents! They might just send one back to you!

It was so darb, and you missed it! Mom's cousin took us out in his jalopy to the new movie palace, and we saw a talkie! Then we went to a really keen drug store and got ice cream sundaes for everyone. It was the cat's meow! Dad says next time you visit, we can take you, too. So no lollygagging— come back soon!

Your Twenties Family

TO:

Time Traveler
Anytown, U.S.A.

TRAVEL FAST FORWARD. Go to page 14 and ride the Time Line back to the present. You can use your ticket to return again and again.
Ta-ta, time traveler!